Everything You Need to Know About

SKIN CARE

Daily cleansing is necessary for healthy-looking skin.

• THE NEED TO KNOW LIBRARY •

Everything You Need to Know About

SKIN CARE

Jane Hammerslough

THE ROSEN PUBLISHING GROUP, INC.
NEW YORK

Published in 1994 by The Rosen Publishing Group, Inc.
29 East 21st Street, New York, NY 10010

First Edition
Copyright 1994 by The Rosen Publishing Group, Inc.

Printed in Canada

Library of Congress Cataloging-in-Publication Data

Hammerslough, Jane.
    Everything you need to know about skin care / Jane
Hammerslough—1st ed.
       p.   cm. — (The Need to know library)
    Includes bibliographical references and index.
    ISBN 0-8239-1686-3
    1. Skin—Care and hygiene—Juvenile literature. [1.Skin—Care
and hygiene.] I. Title. II. Series.
RC87.H294   1994
616.5—dc20   93-45386
                                               CIP
                                               AC

Contents

Introduction 6

1. What Is Skin? 9

2. Great Skin from the Inside Out 15

3. Your Type of Skin 25

4. Skin Problems and Solutions 35

5. Good Habits for Great Skin 41

6. Caring for Your Hands, Knees,
   Elbows, and Feet 47

7. Taking Care of Other Skin Conditions 53

8. At-Home Skin-Care Recipes 57

Glossary—*Explaining New Words* 61

For Further Reading 62

Index 63

Introduction

Clear, glowing skin makes you look great. And looking great can help you *feel* good—about your appearance and about yourself.

For most of us, having great skin depends on the care we give it. It depends on the food we eat, and on the way we live. Healthy skin is one part of a healthy body. Just as a steady diet of junk food isn't good for your body, it is also not good for your skin. Using drugs or alcohol or smoking cigarettes isn't good for your skin or body, either. All of these things affect your health and your appearance.

The way you live affects how good your skin looks. Too little sleep can make it look flat and dull. Living with too much stress and not taking care of yourself can cause breakouts and premature aging. Little or no exercise can also damage your skin. You can control these factors in your life. Your skin will look better as your habits become healthier.

Other things, which you can't control, can also affect the way your skin looks. Environmental factors, like smog and other pollution, can cause blemishes. The sun, which can sometimes help clear up skin, can seriously harm it, too. Overexposure to wind and cold can also damage your skin. Although it is hard to escape these factors, you *can* develop a habit of cleansing your skin and protecting it from damage.

During your teenage years your body goes through many changes that can affect the way your skin looks. Puberty causes your body to start producing hormones that trigger organs and glands to prepare for adulthood. Your skin may become more oily, and more prone to breakouts. Or you may develop "combination" skin, with one area of your skin dry while other parts are oily.

As you mature it can be difficult to deal with the changes in both your skin and the rest of your body. But you can look and feel better if you invest a little of your time each day to take care of your skin. Beginning a skin-care program while you are in your teens can help your skin look its best now—and in the future.

This book will help explain what your skin really is, and how you can have the best-looking skin possible. It will help you learn what type of skin you have, show you how to eat right, and give you ideas for cleansing and protecting your skin. It will tell you what habits are good—and bad—for your skin and your complexion.

This book will also explain how to deal with breakouts and other skin problems, and will offer suggestions on caring for the skin on your hands, feet, scalp, and other areas. There are even recipes for all-natural skin-care preparations that you can make at home.

You *can* work to make your skin look its best. This book will help you put your "best face forward" from now on.

Chapter **1**

What Is Skin?

Skin is the protective covering of your body. It protects your internal organs from damage and bacteria that can cause infections. It regulates your body's temperature. And skin, through the sense of touch, sends messages to your brain about pain and other sensations.

The skin is a dynamic organ, constantly being replenished. By its texture, color, temperature, and clarity, your skin gives information about your general health.

Different Kinds of Skin

Different parts of your body have different kinds of skin. Some skin is thick and durable, like the skin on your elbows, knees, and the soles of your feet. Other skin is thin and delicate, such as the skin on your eyelids or under your arms.

9

Skin is made up of two layers. *Dermis* is the inner layer of skin just below the surface. Nerves, sweat glands, and the "roots" (or *follicles*) of hair are found in the dermis. Each tiny hair that covers your skin has a gland that secretes oil, or *sebum*, which helps keep the skin soft and flexible.

The outer layer of skin that we see is called the *epidermis*. *Pores* are tiny "holes" that can be seen in the skin's epidermis. Pores allow perspiration to leave your body through the skin.

Perspiration allows your body to cool itself. When you are hot, your body produces sweat, which evaporates on the surface of your skin. As the sweat dries, your skin becomes cooler.

This cooling process is very important. It keeps your body at the right temperature. But the sweat that leaves your body can attract grime and can block pores. This can cause a number of skin problems.

The oil that is *secreted*, or released, from your body through your skin is important. Oil keeps your skin soft. It protects your skin from wind, cold, and other elements. But oil can also clog your pores, attract dirt, and cause blemishes.

The Skin of a Teen

When you enter your teens, your body goes through many changes. The onset of puberty starts the production of hormones in the adolescent. These hormones trigger glands and organs

CROSS SECTION OF HUMAN SKIN

(Enlarged)

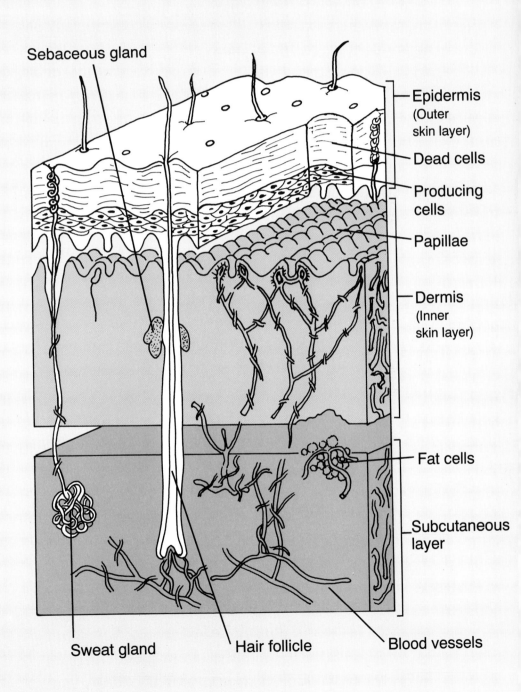

Sebaceous gland

Epidermis
(Outer
skin layer)

Dead cells

Producing
cells

Papillae

Dermis
(Inner
skin layer)

Fat cells

Subcutaneous
layer

Sweat gland

Hair follicle

Blood vessels

to produce certain oils and other chemicals. Your skin may become more oily, and begin to look shiny and feel greasy, especially in the "T-zone"— the area across your forehead, and down over your nose and chin.

Because of these changes during adolescence, you may develop blackheads, pimples, and other blemishes even if you have never had any skin problems before. Your face, neck, back, shoulders, and chest may all be affected by the oil being produced by your body.

You can help your skin look its best with careful cleansing every day. It is very important to be gentle with your skin. Scrubbing your skin too hard, or using products that dry your skin, may seem like a good idea, but doing this can encourage your body to produce *more* oil. It can actually make your skin look worse.

Sitting in the sun to dry the excess oil from your skin might also seem like a good idea. But the heat from the sun dries the epidermis, while stimulating more oil production in the dermis. Research has shown that in the last few decades, the sun has become even more dangerous to human skin. This is because of loss to the ozone layer. The ozone layer is a layer of gases in the atmosphere that reduces the harmful rays of the sun. As this layer has been reduced, the ultraviolet rays of the sun have become more dangerous. Long hours of sun worship can make your skin problems worse.

Long hours of sun tanning can also cause wrinkles and serious medical problems such as skin cancer.

When your body produces less oil, your skin becomes dry. Overdryness takes the "glow" away from your skin, making the top layer look ashy, flaky, and wrinkled. During the winter months your skin can more easily become dry. Exposure to cold, dry wind outdoors can make your skin chapped. Hot, dry air indoors can also *dehydrate*, or take moisture from, your skin.

Later in this book, we'll look at how you can cleanse and protect your skin to keep it looking its best. But first, we'll look at beautiful skin from the inside out. Because what you eat can make a big difference in how you look.

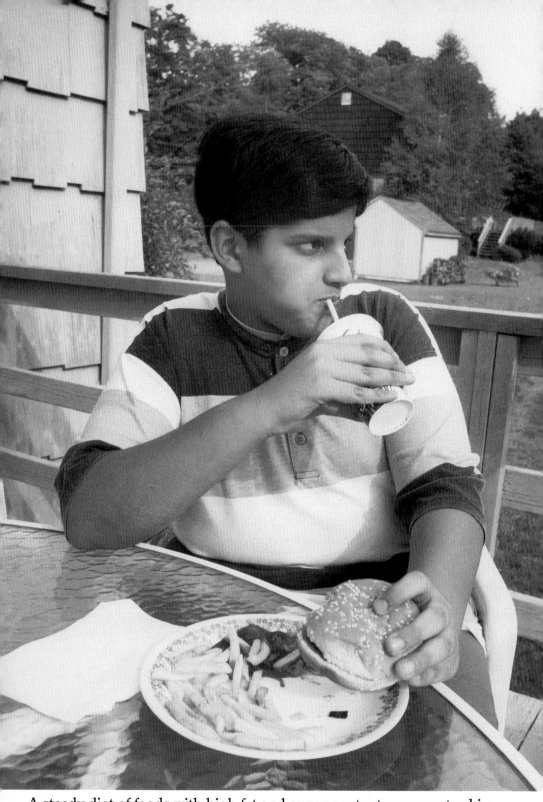

A steady diet of foods with high fat and sugar content may create skin problems.

Chapter 2

Great Skin from the Inside Out

When it comes to the way your skin looks, you really are what you eat! Maintaining a healthy, balanced diet is one of the most important things you can do to have healthy-looking, beautiful skin.

You have probably heard many opinions about what you should (or shouldn't) eat to have great skin. How much do you know about which foods are really good—and which are not good for your skin? Take this Food Facts and Fiction Quiz and find out:

TRUE OR FALSE
1. Donuts, french fries, and other fried foods cause acne.
2. Salt can affect the condition of your skin.

15

3. You need fat in your diet to look your best.

4. Chocolate is very bad for your complexion.

5. Drinking water doesn't hurt your skin, but it doesn't help it either.

6. Caffeine does not affect your skin.

7. You need to have certain vitamins and minerals every day to look your best.

ANSWERS

1. False. Although in the past people believed that eating oily foods could cause acne (serious skin-scarring from pimples), doctors now believe that this is not true. Acne is caused by excess oil produced far below the surface of the skin, which can cause clogging of your pores and inflammation. True acne must be treated by a doctor with medications that work under the skin's surface. *Eating* food with oil does not generally affect the production of oil in skin. However, a well-balanced diet can help your skin's tone and condition.

Touching your face, especially after you have eaten greasy foods, can contribute to blemishes. If you eat fried foods, wash your hands promptly.

You may develop an allergy or sensitivity to fried or other foods, which can affect your skin. If you seem to experience frequent breakouts after eating these foods, avoid them.

2. True. Salt contains iodine, which can irritate pores. To help your skin look its best, avoid eating too many salty snacks.

Fresh fruits and vegetables are important in a well-balanced diet.

Skin eruptions may signal the need to adjust nutrition and/or hygiene.

3. True. Believe it or not. Some fat is necessary in a healthy diet, to help keep skin soft. Very low-calorie or "no-fat" diets can actually cause your skin to become dry and even cracked. Watch your cholesterol by choosing "healthy" fats like olive and corn oil.

4. False. Although eating chocolate will not improve the way your skin looks, it generally does not do it any harm, either. Chocolate contains a large amount of caffeine, which can make you jumpy and prevent you from getting enough sleep. A lack of sleep can affect the way your skin looks. However, eating chocolate in moderation usually does not have any impact on your skin.

5. False. Drinking water can help your skin, by helping it rid itself of impurities and providing moisture. Several glasses of water a day can help your skin become clearer. If you live in a dry environment, try misting your skin with water to ease dryness.

6. False. Too much caffeine can disturb your sleep and make your skin look lifeless. To look your best, try not to have any caffeine after 6 p.m. Caffeine can also block your body's ability to absorb iron, a mineral especially important to young women. Caffeine is found in coffee, tea, many sodas, and chocolate.

7. True. Your skin is an organ, and just like other organs in your body, it requires daily nutrition to function well.

How Can You Eat to Look Your Best?

Let's take a look at the four major food groups:

DAIRY products provide calcium (for strong bones, teeth, and nails), protein, and riboflavin. Four daily servings are recommended for people ages 11 to 24.

Sample servings:

One cup of milk (skim, lowfat, or whole)
One cup of yogurt
One ounce of cheese

FRUITS AND VEGETABLES provide vitamins, minerals, sugar for energy, and fiber. Four to five servings are recommended daily.

Sample servings:

Leafy green and yellow vegetables, like broccoli, spinach, and squash. One or more cups recommended daily.

Citrus fruits, tomatoes, and other salad greens. One or more servings (one medium-sized whole fruit, one cup of vegetables, or one cup of juice) recommended every day.

Potatoes, corn, apples, grapes, bananas, and other fruits and vegetables.

PROTEIN products (meat, fish, poultry, tofu, dried beans, and peas) supply niacin, iron, thiamine, and protein for cell growth. Two servings recommended daily.

Sample servings:

Two to three ounces of meat, fish, chicken, turkey, or tofu.

One cup of peas or beans.

GRAIN products (breads, cereals, pasta, and rice) provide carbohydrates (for slow-burning energy), thiamine, iron, niacin, and some fiber. Four to six servings recommended daily.

Sample servings:

1/4 cup of cereal
One slice of bread
1/2 cup cooked rice or pasta
1/2 medium bagel or muffin

Nutrition Tips

• To get the most out of your diet, opt for fresh fruits and vegetables instead of canned or frozen. Cooking can cause vegetables and fruits to lose vitamins. Try to eat at least a couple of servings raw (salads, juices, etc.) each day.

• Whole grains are more nutritious than processed grains. Try whole wheat breads and pasta and brown rice to get the best nutrition.

• Beta carotene, found in green leafy and other vegetables, is an excellent internal "cleaner" of your skin. It helps your body get rid of harmful impurities caused by air and other pollution.

• Calcium is very important to growing teens. Milk products, spinach, and canned salmon or sardines with bones are all good sources of calcium. (You can also try calcium-enriched orange juice.)

• Iron is also important to growing bodies. Iron-rich foods include meat, poultry, fish, peas and beans, raisins and other dried fruits, and leafy greens.

• Growing teens require an average of 2,000 to 3,000 calories a day—depending on height and rate of activity—in order to stay healthy. Experts recommend limiting total fat intake to no more than 30 percent of your total calorie intake. For teenagers, that equals 73 grams per day, which can be found in meats, oils, and butter. While you need some fat in your diet to stay healthy, before you reach for a

Monitor the time you expose your skin to direct sun and always use a protective sunscreen of some kind.

cookie or candy bar, check out the number of fat grams! You may be surprised at how much fat can be found in most sweets and salty snacks.

• Drink between six and eight glasses of water throughout the day. It can help keep your skin moist and help clean out impurities.

Stress and lack of sleep may cause skin to look pale and lifeless.

Chapter 3

Your Type of Skin

Like fingerprints, everyone has a complexion that is uniquely their own. Some people have facial skin that's oily, others have skin that tends to be dry. And some people have skin that is dry in some places and oily in others. Your age, family history, and environment can all influence your *skin type*.

Knowing your skin type, and learning about the best products to cleanse, tone, and moisturize is important to having your skin look its very best. Products that make one type of skin look great can do nothing at all for another type of skin.

What's your skin type? Check these profiles to find out:

Your skin type is *oily* if...

- your pores are visible or large

Each skin type requires specific care.

- your skin frequently looks shiny
- you have blackheads or blemishes frequently
- you have few visible lines
- your skin rarely feels dry

Your skin type is *dry* if...
- your pores are not at all noticeable
- your skin tends to feel tight or dry
- your skin flakes or chaps easily
- you rarely have blackheads or blemishes
- you have some fine lines visible

Your skin type is *normal/combination* if...
- the pores on your T-zone are noticeable, but those on your cheeks are not
- you have occasional blackheads or breakouts
- your T-zone skin looks shiny sometimes
- your skin sometimes feels dry or tight, especially in the cheek area

Other things can affect your skin's appearance, such as heredity, ethnicity, and environment. Here are some common conditions and ways to make your specific kind of skin look great:

Sensitive skin is a condition that can affect oily, dry, or normal/combination skin. If you have sensitive skin, your complexion is irritated easily. You may be allergic to certain kinds of cleansing products, makeup, moisturizers, and even sunscreens. Look for *hypoallergenic* products. These are products that do not contain fragrance or other possible skin irritants. They are especially designed for sensitive, allergy-prone skin.

Black/African-American skin tends to be very sensitive, so it should be treated very gently. Some conditions that frequently affect black skin include *hyperpigmentation* and *hypopigmentation*. These can both make skin color look uneven. Squeezing or rough handling of your face can cause or worsen these conditions.

Keloids are dark raised bumps that occur on dark skin. They are actually scar tissue, also caused by scrubbing and squeezing the skin.

Dryness can make black skin look ashy and dull. Treat the skin gently and use plenty of moisturizers, especially during the winter, when skin is at its driest.

Very fair, white skin can be of any type, and it can be particularly sensitive. Fair skin tends to sunburn and chap easily. Treat it gently and use sunscreen liberally whenever you are exposed to the sun.

Other skin types can also vary a great deal. Koreans, Japanese, Chinese, and other people of Far Eastern ancestry tend to have sensitive, light skin that needs protection from the sun and wind. Asian Indians and many Hispanics have darker skin that tends to withstand direct sun better than white skin. As a general rule, the lighter the skin, the more sensitive it will be to sunburn and chapping from wind.

Smoking can affect the tone and health of the skin.

Taking Care of Your Type of Skin

According to Kathleen Walas, International Beauty and Fashion Director at Avon Products, gentle cleansing is best for skin. For all skin types, Ms. Walas recommends a two-step process using cleansers and toners.

Cleansers remove dirt, perspiration, soot, and other pollution and makeup from the surface of your skin. Cleansers include soaps, lotions, creams, and gels. Use a cleanser and lukewarm water to wash your face; too-hot water can dry your skin. And use a gentle touch—scrubbing can irritate the skin, worsen existing problems, and even cause premature wrinkles. When you are finished cleansing, be sure to rinse carefully, removing all remaining residue of cleanser.

After washing, Ms. Walas recommends using *toners*, which are also sometimes called fresheners. Toners are applied to a cottonball, skin whisked over your face to remove the last traces of cleanser. Toners can be mild, for normal/combination or dry skin, or astringent, for oily skin. Astringent toners work to get rid of excess oil and "plump up" the skin surrounding pores to make them look smaller.

Moisturizers, which help replenish water in the skin, can help make almost all skin types look their best. Apply moisturizing creams and lotions while skin is clean and slightly damp; it will help "seal in" moisture. If your skin tends to be oily, look for oil-free, water-based moisturizers.

A facial once or twice a week will help to revitalize your skin.

WHICH PRODUCTS ARE BEST FOR YOUR SKIN TYPE?

SKIN TYPE	CLEANSER	TONER	MOISTURIZER
Normal/ Combination	Mild soap, non-soap cleanser or light lotion; in hotter months use soap on T-Zone to take care of oiliness.	Gentle or mild toner; use astringent on T-Zone when needed.	Use lightweight moisterizer daily on dry areas like cheeks and neck. In cold months, use a more heavyweight moisterizer.
Oily	Oil-balancing soap or lotion, or glycerine (transparent) soap.	Astringent to handle excess oil. Products containing salicylic acid can help get rid of dead skin cells.	Use water-based moisterizer on dry areas only, twice daily.
Dry	Milky cleanser or cleansing cream or moisturizing, nonsoap beauty bar.	Mild toner or refresher without alcohol.	Rich lotion or cream used morning and night.

Using *exfoliants*, which are also called scrubs, cleansing grains, or masks, removes dead skin cells that can dull your complexion. Depending on your skin type, exfoliating once or twice a week can help get rid of cells that can clog pores and trigger breakouts, and "renew" your skin. Using exfoliants requires extra gentle treatment. Don't try to scrub the grains into your skin; instead, apply the exfoliant and very lightly massage your face for just a few seconds. The result will be fresher-looking, undamaged skin.

A note on makeup: There is a wide variety of makeup and cosmetic products on the market today. Makeup can be used for a number of skin-care purposes. First, it can be used to cover up blemishes or unevenness in the complexion. Second, it can be used to highlight certain features or to make others seem less noticeable. Third, some makeup products that contain moisturizers can be used to help the skin retain its moisture. Finally, some makeup even contains sunscreen or sunblock that can protect skin from the harmful effects of being outside a great deal.

Always read labels carefully before buying and using medications for the skin.

Chapter 4

Skin Problems and Solutions

Nobody has perfect skin, not even models and movie stars. Nearly everyone has an occasional blemish. How do you take care of minor skin problems *before* they become major skin problems?

Zapping Zits and Blemishes

Blackheads are pores that have become clogged with oil or dirt. The "plug" that forms in the pore is called a *comedo*. When the comedo is exposed to air, it turns dark or black, causing a blackhead. If the plug is under the surface of the skin, and not exposed to air, a *whitehead* (pimple or "zit") forms.

You can clean out blackheads by first washing your face with warm water, which will help soften the comedo. Then, *very gently* press out the contents of the pore. Splash cold water on the affected spot to close the pore.

If a whitehead forms, it is best not to squeeze the skin. "Popping" whiteheads can make the whitehead worse and cause infection and scarring. Use tinted, medicated cover-up to hide pimples until they disappear on their own.

To help speed the healing process, beauty expert Kathleen Walas recommends steaming the skin. Boil enough water to fill a large bowl up halfway. Drape a towel over your head to form a "tent." Bend over the bowl, letting the steam open your pores. Don't get too close—the steam is very hot and can burn.

While pores are still open, apply a cotton ball soaked in very warm salt water to the pimple. (You can make the salt water by dissolving one teaspoon of salt in two cups of water.) Hold the cotton ball against the whitehead for about three minutes. Ms. Walas recommends repeating the salt water treatment several times a day.

To take away the redness and soreness that often accompany whiteheads, Ms. Walas recommends using ice. Place two ice cubes in a plastic bag and hold against the affected spot for a few minutes. Repeat as needed.

To avoid getting blackheads and whiteheads, look for cosmetics and moisturizers that are labeled "non-comedogenic." That means that they are specially designed not to clog pores.

Some over-the-counter medications can also help blemishes. Look for medicated creams and lotions containing *benzoyl peroxide*, which can dry up excess oil. To help heal pimples and prevent new blemishes from forming, look for products containing *salicylic acid*, which can help your skin get rid of dead skin cells that can clog pores.

Dealing with Acne

Acne is a skin condition that most often affects teens. It can be painful and difficult to live with. Unlike ordinary blackheads or pimples that can drain and dry out as they are exposed to air, acne is caused by excess oil and infection deep within the skin. Because these infected pimples can often not drain, they become painful and inflamed. Serious acne can result in scarring of the skin as well.

If your acne is not severe, paying attention to your diet, cleansing, and choice of cosmetics can help. Because some acne can be triggered by stress or exhaustion, working out ways to deal with pressure and getting enough rest can also help. If breakouts are very frequent, and acne is severe and painful, it is best to see a *dermatologist*. This is a doctor who specializes in treating skin problems.

Other Minor Skin Troubles

Extreme dryness or rashes can be caused by heredity, the environment, or certain products such as detergents, cosmetics, or even fabrics. If you experience dryness or rashes after using certain products or wearing certain fabrics, it may be an

Gentle washing removes dirt and excess oils from face.

allergic reaction. See a dermatologist if you continue to have problems.

Dandruff is a condition that affects the skin on your scalp, causing it to flake. Try using a medicated shampoo containing coal tar or laurel sulfate, and be sure to rinse extra thoroughly. Sometimes shampooing a little less often than usual can help relieve a dandruff problem.

Sunburn is a painful and all-too-common skin problem for teens. Avoid sunburning by wearing sunblock with a Sun Protection Factor (SPF) of at least 15. Make sure that your sunscreen products are all waterproof, so the protection will remain even if you get wet. If you do get sunburned, relieve the pain with aloe vera gel, available at drugstores and health food stores.

Moles, while usually harmless, can occasionally cause problems. If you notice a change in the size, shape, or color of a mole, consult a doctor. Moles can be removed by a dermatologist for cosmetic reasons.

Warts are harmless bumps that are caused by a virus. Although they are harmless and usually disappear within days, they are contagious to the touch.

Skin tags are similar to moles. They are most often tiny, harmless bumps that stick out in a narrow "tubelike" shape. Unlike moles, many skin tags are skin-colored or very light in color.

Healthy-looking skin adds to the sense of well-being.

Chapter 5

Good Habits for Great Skin

It's a fact: healthy living means healthy-looking skin. Not surprisingly, habits that are bad for the rest of your body can also be bad for your looks. Drugs, smoking, too little sleep, and too much stress can cause breakouts, premature aging, and dull, lifeless skin.

Smoking and Your Skin

Most people know that *smoking* is bad for your lungs and heart. But did you know that the nicotine in cigarettes can make your skin look dull? Nicotine causes the blood vessels in the face to constrict (get smaller), limiting the amount of oxygen that reaches the skin. The reduced blood circulation from smoking can lead to puffiness under the eyes and early wrinkling.

Smoking can also rob your body of vitamins C and B, both important for your skin. The best way to avoid the bad effects of smoking on your skin is either to quit smoking or never start.

Drugs and Alcohol Are Dangerous

Using *drugs*—marijuana, amphetamines, narcotics, cocaine—will severely hurt your body and your mind in many ways. Drugs can also hurt your skin, causing poor color and tone. Drugs can depress your appetite so you don't get proper nutrients. And drugs can lead to sleeplessness, which can cause blemishes. In addition to ruining general health and appearance, many drugs will threaten life. Injecting certain drugs, for example, greatly increases the risk of AIDS, hepatitis, and other dangerous diseases.

Using *alcohol* can also affect the way your skin looks. Excessive alcohol use can lead to broken capillaries (blood vessels) in the skin, making it look red. Alcohol can also rob your body of important vitamins and minerals and can dehydrate your skin.

Sleep, Stress, and Your Skin

Not everyone requires the same amount of sleep. But getting enough sleep can be a big factor in your skin's appearance. When you are tired, the blood in your body is directed toward your muscles and organs and away from your face, making it *look* tired. Bags under the eyes, puffiness, and lackluster tone can also appear. Additionally, not getting enough sleep can trigger breakouts and make dry skin drier. Teenagers should try to get at least seven hours of sleep each night—it can make a big difference in how you look.

Stress and not getting enough sleep often go together. Both can hurt your complexion. Stress can make you look tired, and can even cause premature aging.

Everyone experiences stress at times. Working out ways to handle stress can make a positive difference in your life—and in your complexion!

To handle stress, try making lists of the things that are causing the stress in your life. Number them according to their importance. Next, make a list of things that you can do to deal with the stress.

Make an effort to try to relax when you are tense—close your eyes and imagine a beautiful place, a great song, or a good friend. Take a warm bath or a hot shower to relax tensed-up muscles. Sit down and take slow, deep breaths for ten or fifteen minutes.

Exercise is another positive way of dealing with stress that can also improve your skin. Exercise can improve energy, allowing you to handle stress better. And regularly working out by playing sports, doing aerobics, running, walking, dancing, or swimming improves circulation, which gives the skin a rosy glow.

Sun: Friend or Foe?

Beginning good habits for great skin as early as possible will affect how your skin looks now, and in the future. Studies show that sunburns during teenage years can result in wrinkling during the years ahead. Plan to have beautiful skin for your *entire* life by taking precautions against sun damage *now*.

Many dermatologists recommend wearing sunscreen every day, applying it in the morning as you would moisturizer. The only effective, long-term way to combat wrinkles is to prevent them from forming. Starting early can be your best defense for the future.

In the past, people believed that tanning could help acne. However, experts now believe that tanning merely provides a camouflage for blemish-prone skin. While exposure to the sun dries out the top layer of skin, it can also encourage the production of *more* oil, and can worsen skin problems. In addition, prolonged exposure to the sun can cause other problems for people taking some anti-acne medications. Talk with a dermatologist about how much time you should spend in the sun if you have acne.

Shaving

For most people, shaving irritates the skin. Because men and women traditionally shave different parts of their bodies, different areas become

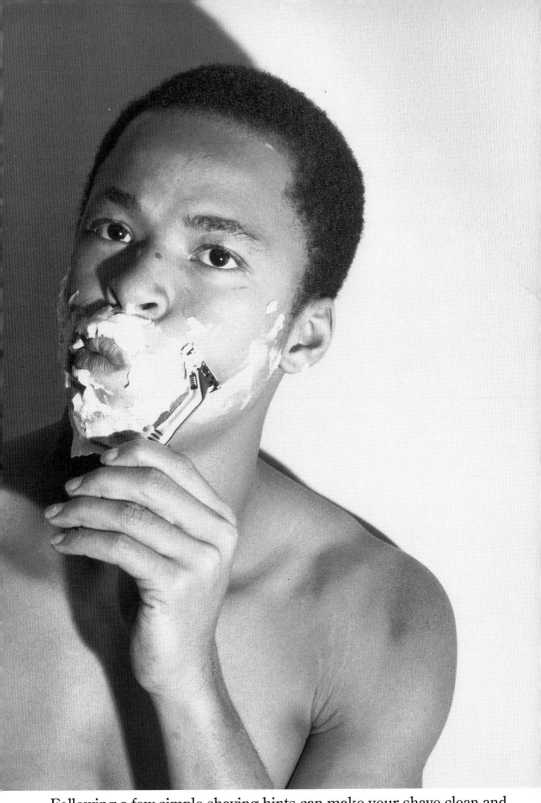

Following a few simple shaving hints can make your shave clean and comfortable.

irritated for men and women. Here are several
general tips on shaving with a blade:

• Prepare skin for shaving by applying warm
water or by taking a warm shower or bath. Warm
water opens the pores of the skin and makes for a
more comfortable shave.

• Use only sharp blades. Dull blades can cause
irritation and can cause extra cutting of the skin.

• Keep the blade clean by continuously rinsing
in cold water while you shave. A clean blade will
shave more effectively and a cool blade will reduce
friction that can cause irritation while shaving.

• Wash shaved areas well after shaving. Film
left behind from soap or shaving cream can cause
dryness and itching.

• Creams and moisturizers can soothe irritated
skin after shaving, especially lotions with aloe.
Apply these lotions gently and do not use too
much. Using too much cream or lotion can clog
pores.

• Electric razors are another choice. Although
they do not require shaving cream, they can cause
more irritation to the skin than regular blades.
Because everybody's skin is different, try shaving
by different methods to see which works best for
you.

Chapter 6

Caring for Your Hands, Knees, Elbows, and Feet

The skin on your hands, knees, elbows, and feet is not as delicate as the skin on your face. Still, like the skin on your face, the other skin on your body can look its best with a regular skin-care program.

Your hands express a lot about you. Like the skin on your face, the skin on your hands is constantly exposed to the elements, as well as to dirt and detergents. The skin on hands can easily become dry, chapped, and wrinkly. Your nails, too, can become dry and brittle. But with a little care, it is easy to make your hands soft and smooth, and your nails strong and hard.

47

Helping Hands

Detergents are found in dishwashing liquid and other household cleansers as well as in some soaps and shampoos. While detergents can clean thoroughly, they can also remove moisture from your skin, leaving it feeling dry. To protect your hands, wear rubber gloves when you wash dishes. Choose detergent-free soaps to clean your hands, and apply lotion frequently.

Are your nails brittle or dry? Weak or soft? Your heredity and diet may be to blame. Some people have weak nails naturally. Extreme weight-loss diets can reduce the level of protein, calcium, and vitamin A that your body needs for strong, beautiful nails. To help your nails look their best, keep track of what you eat and keep your nails clean and well trimmed.

Other good habits can help you have beautiful hands now and in the future. Start doing these things while you are young and you won't have to worry about the appearance and feel of your hands as you age:

• Always wear gloves in cold weather. You'll be more comfortable (many people believe that when your hands are warm your whole body stays warmer), and your hands will be protected.

• When you're outside in the sun, don't forget sunscreen for your hands. It will prevent tiny, dry lines from forming, and help you avoid "shoe leather" hands when you're older.

Soaking hands in a gentle cleanser will soften skin and help to clean fingernails.

Regular manicures can help the way your hands look. And they're not just for women anymore! Manicures have become popular for men who know that hand and nail care are an important part of good grooming. Go to a professional or try this do-it-yourself manicure:

- Wash your hands, then smooth on skin cream.
- Women: Remove old nail polish.
- File your nails gently with a fine emery board, in one direction only. ("Sawing" the nails can cause splitting and other damage.)
- Soak your hands for several minutes in warm water. Dry hands, and very gently push back your cuticles with a washcloth or a cotton swab. Don't push back too far.
- Massage cream into hands and cuticles.
- Wipe off excess cream.

To smooth dry hands, try an overnight treatment. Before you go to bed, slather rich cream on your hands, then wear a pair of cotton gloves overnight. In the morning, your hands will be soft.

Putting Your Best Feet Forward

Your feet work hard for you! Make them look—and feel—good with some special care.

Here are some "foot fixers" that can help tired, achy feet:

- Soak feet in a warm bath to relax. Add bath or mineral oil to the water to soften skin. Soap feet, then gently use a pumice stone to scrub away rough dead skin.

• For extra tingle after a long, hard day, add two tablespoons of Epsom salts to warm water in a large tub. Soak feet and relax.

• Dry feet thoroughly after a soak or shower. Use cornstarch-based dusting powder to help prevent foot odor.

• Trim toenails carefully. They should be cut straight across, but not too short or they may curve under and become ingrown.

• Corns, which are painful callus-like bumps on toes and other areas, are most often caused by too-tight shoes. Choose shoes with care to get the best fit. To soften and get rid of corns, use commercially available corn pads. To prevent corns and other minor irritations such as blisters and rashes, take care always to wear comfortable shoes, clean socks, and to bathe your feet regularly.

• Choose all-cotton socks that absorb perspiration and help feet "breathe." Synthetics can trap perspiration and cause odor.

• Help relax feet by doing "toe crunches." Spread the toes apart and wiggle them, then point them. Repeat ten times.

• Massaging your feet for a few minutes each day not only feels good, but can help improve circulation. Using both hands, begin with each toe and work back to your heels. Massage the balls of your feet and instep firmly but gently.

Getting to Elbows and Knees

Elbows and knees need attention, too. The skin in these places can become tough and leathery. To keep elbows and knees looking smooth, try these tips:

• In the bath, use oil to soften elbows and knees and massage gently with a washcloth to remove dead, dry skin.

• Cut a lemon in half and squeeze out juice. Place an elbow on each lemon half and rest for ten minutes. Wash off your elbows and apply moisturizing cream.

• In cold or dry weather, rub petroleum jelly (such as Vaseline) into clean elbows and knees to soften and seal in moisture.

Chapter 7

Taking Care of Other Skin Conditions

Nobody's perfect. Everyone is occasionally bothered by small skin problems. The following is a run-down of some common complaints and what you can do about them.

Warts

Warts are hard, raised lumps on the skin that can be unattractive. No, warts are not caused by touching frogs! Warts are actually caused by a virus, and there are many ways to get rid of them. Try salicylic-acid-based remedies found in drug stores.

Some people swear by home folk remedies to get rid of warts. These include rubbing the wart three times a day with a gold ring, covering the

wart with a bandage until it disappears, and applying a paste made of salt and water to the wart three
times a day. They might be worth a try if other
remedies don't work for you.

Plantar Warts

These are painful spots found on the bottom of
your feet. Try using over-the-counter medicine
that is formulated especially to get rid of plantar
warts. If you get no relief, see a doctor to get rid
of them.

Moles

Nearly everyone has moles. Moles are brown,
blue, black, or flesh-colored spots on the skin that
contain a high amount of a skin coloring, or pigment, called *melanin*. They can be raised or have
hair growing out of them. Never pluck the hair on
moles; it can cause infection. If a mole is very
unsightly, it can be removed by a dermatologist.
Most moles are harmless. However, if you notice
that a mole enlarges, changes shape or color, be-
gins to bleed, itch, or cause pain, you should see a
doctor.

Freckles

Freckles are also concentrations of melanin in
the skin. Exposure to the sun tends to "bring out"
freckles. Always wear sunscreen if you wish to
avoid getting more freckles.

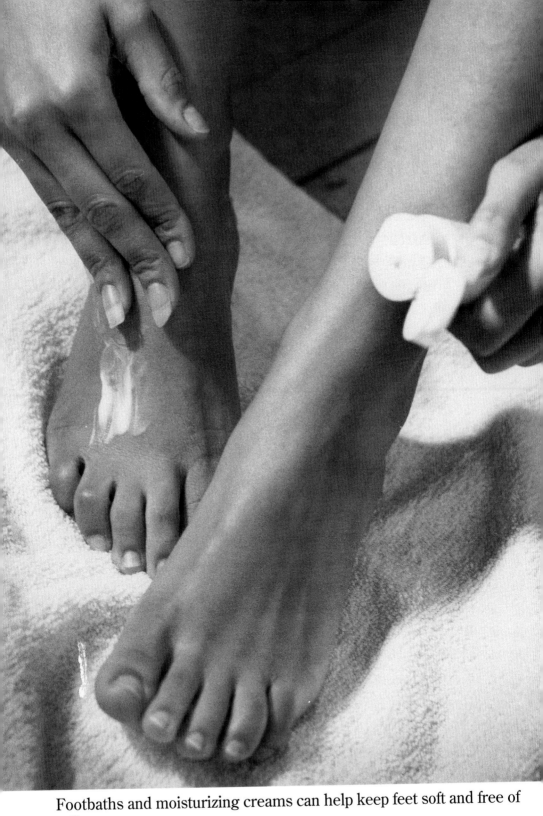

Footbaths and moisturizing creams can help keep feet soft and free of calluses.

Athlete's Foot

Athlete's foot is caused by a fungus infection, and can cause pain and itching, usually between the toes. It is highly contagious, and you can pick it up in changing rooms, public swimming pool locker rooms, and other public places. Avoid athlete's foot by keeping feet clean, cool, and dry. You can treat athlete's foot with anti-fungal products (creams and powders) found at the pharmacy, or see a doctor.

Calluses, Corns, and Blisters

Calluses, corns, and blisters on the feet are mostly caused by shoes that don't fit properly. Soak your feet to soften calluses, then rub with a pumice stone. Use medicated pads to relieve pain and clear up corns. Keep blisters clean and dry, covering them if needed. If they do not go away in a reasonable amount of time, see a doctor.

Chapter **8**

At-Home Skin-Care Recipes

No matter what your skin type, you can make all-natural skin care treatments at home—for only pennies! Most of the following "recipes" use ingredients found in your kitchen. (Remember that if you are allergic to *eating* certain foods, using them on your skin will probably cause problems as well. Use common sense when making homemade treatments.)

Cleansing Masks

Ready to give yourself a facial? Cleansing masks are a good way to help skin with too much or too little oil.

For *oily* skin try a mask made by following either one of these steps.

• Mix a tablespoon of plain yogurt (don't use the sweetened kind) with ground almonds and a squeeze of lemon or lime juice until a thin paste forms. Apply to face and massage very gently. Rinse.

• Mix two tablespoons of oatmeal with a little orange juice until a paste forms. Apply to face and relax for 10 minutes. Rinse off with cool water.

For *normal* skin:

• Pound the flesh of a small cucumber and add one tablespoon of milk. Add enough oatmeal to make a paste, then apply to face. Leave on for 10 minutes, then rinse.

• Exfoliate your skin with salt! Lather your hands with your favorite soap, then add 1/2 teaspoon of table salt to the lather. Gently rub over your face for one minute. Rinse carefully.

For *dry* skin:

• Mash half an avocado and apply to dry areas. Leave on for 10 minutes, then rinse.

• Apply a beaten egg to face. Let dry. Rinse very carefully!

For *all* types of skin:

• Mash half a banana with a tablespoon of honey. Add oatmeal until it forms a paste. Apply to skin for 15 minutes. Rinse off.

There are many homemade formulas that are inexpensive and useful in caring for the skin.

Toners

- Mix two tablespoons of rose water with 1/2 cup of mineral water for a refreshing toner for all skin types.
- Mix two tablespoons of witch hazel with two tablespoons of prepared camomile tea. Apply with a cotton ball after cleansing.

Other Skin-Care Secrets

- To help tired-looking eyes, soak two teabags in cold water and place over eyes for 10 minutes. Cold cucumber slices may be used as well. Eyes will look and feel refreshed.
- Use a small dab of petroleum jelly on lips to protect from chapping, on eyelashes to moisturize and thicken, and on heels and other areas to soften.
- Use grapeseed or almond oil to seal in moisture after a shower or bath.

Now that you know the many things you can do to maintain and improve your skin, the rest is up to you. Just remember that your skin covers your entire body and looking great means having great-looking skin!

Glossary—*Explaining New Words*

acne A common skin disease among adolescents causing sometimes painful and unsightly pimples on the face, back, and chest.

adolescence Time of life between puberty and maturity.

dehydrate To remove water or moisture.

dermatologist Doctor who specializes in the treatment of skin conditions.

dermis The inner layer of skin found just below the skin's surface.

epidermis The outer layer or surface of skin.

hyperpigmentation Irritated skin that turns dark, creating an uneven skin tone.

hypoallergenic Term used for products that do not cause allergic reactions, formulated for sensitive skin.

hypopigmentation Light skin patches that make skin tone look uneven.

keloid Dark, raised bump of scar tissue.

pigment Coloring in skin.

pores Tiny holes in skin that allow perspiration and oil to leave the body.

secrete To produce and release a substance by a cell or gland.

T-Zone The T-shaped area on your face across your forehead, and down your nose and chin.

For Further Reading

Jackson, Victoria, and Calistro, Paddy. *Redefining Beauty.* New York: Warner Books, 1993. Further information on skin care and makeup.

Kanner, Catherine. *The Book of the Bath.* New York: Balantine Books, 1985. Fun how-to's and recipes for relaxing and energizing soaks.

Schorr, Lia, and Miller-Sims, Shari. *Lia Schorr's Seasonal Skin Care.* New York: Prentice Hall Press, 1988. Advice on different types of skin care programs from a well-known beauty expert.

Walas, Kathleen. *Real Beauty...Real Women: A Workbook for Making the Best of Your Own Good Looks.* New York: MasterMedia Books, 1992. This book is an overview on taking care of your skin and looking great at any age.

Zeldis, Yona. *Coping with Beauty, Fitness and Fashion: A Girl's Guide.* New York: Rosen Publishing Group, 1987. Just for teens, a guide to eating right and looking good.

Index

Acne, 15–16, 37, 44
AIDS, 42
alcohol (and skin), 6, 42
astringent(s), 30, 32
athlete's foot, 56

Benzoyl peroxide, 37
blackheads, 12, 27, 35–37
blemishes, 7, 10, 12, 16, 27, 35, 36, 42
blisters, 56
breakouts, 7, 8, 27, 33, 41, 43

Caffeine (and skin), 16, 19
calcium, 20, 22, 48
calluses, 56
cleansers, 25, 30
cleansing, 7, 8, 30, 37
comedos, 35
complexion, 8, 16, 27, 33, 43
corns, 51, 56

Dandruff, 39
dehydration (and skin), 13, 42
dermatologist, 37, 39, 44, 54
detergents, 37, 47–48
drugs (and skin), 6, 41, 42

Environment (and skin), 7, 27, 37
epidermis, 9, 12
exercise (and skin), 7, 43
exfoliants, 33, 58
exhaustion (and skin), 37

Facial, 57
fat, 16, 19, 22–23

fiber, 20–21
food groups, 20–21
foot care, 50–51
freckles, 54
fresheners (*see* toners)

Glycerine, 32

Hands, protection for, 48, 50
hepatitis, 42
heredity (and skin), 27, 37
hyperpigmentation, 28
hypoallergenic products, 27
hypopigmentation, 28

Iron, 21–22

Keloids, 28

Makeup, 33
manicures, 50
massages, 51
medicated shampoo (*see* dandruff)
melanin (pigment), 54
moisturizers, 25, 28, 30, 33, 44, 46
moles, 39, 54

Non-comedogenic products, 36
nutrition, tips on, 22–23

Perspiration, 10
pimples, 12, 16, 36, 37
plantar warts, 54
pollution, 7, 22

pores, 9, 16, 27, 30, 33, 35–37
premature aging, 7, 41, 43
protein, 21, 48
puberty, 7, 10
pumice stone, 51, 56

Rashes, 37

Salicylic acid, 32, 37, 53
sebum (oil), 10, 12, 13, 44
shaving, 44–46
skin
   cancer, 13
   definition of, 9
   diet and 15–23, 37
   dry, 7, 13, 25, 27, 30, 43, 52, 58
   normal/combination, 7, 27,
     30, 58
   oily, 7, 25, 27, 30, 58
   sun and, 7, 12–13, 39, 44
   tags, 39

   taking care of, 30–33, 35–39,
     48–52
   types of, 9–10, 25–28
skin-care recipes, 57, 58, 60
smoking (and skin), 6, 29, 41–42
stress (and skin), 7, 37, 41
sunscreens, 23, 27, 28, 33, 39,
    44, 54

Toners, 25, 30
T-zone, 12, 27, 32

Vitamins, 20, 22, 42, 48

Walas, Kathleen, 30, 36
warts, 39, 53–54
water, 16, 19, 23
whiteheads, 35–36 (*see also* pimples)
wrinkles, 13, 30, 41, 44

Zits, 35 (*see also* pimples)

About the Author
Jane Hammerslough is a newspaper columnist who writes about parents and childen. She is the author of many books for young adults, including *Everything You Need to Know About Teen Motherhood*, published by the Rosen Publishing Group, and *The Home Alone Survival Guide*, published by Bantam Books. She has also published four picture books for very young readers. Ms. Hammerslough lives in New York.

Photo Credits
Cover photo: Stuart Rabinowitz.
All other photos: Norma Mondazzi.

Design/Production: Blackbirch Graphics, Inc.

HIGHSMITH 45-200

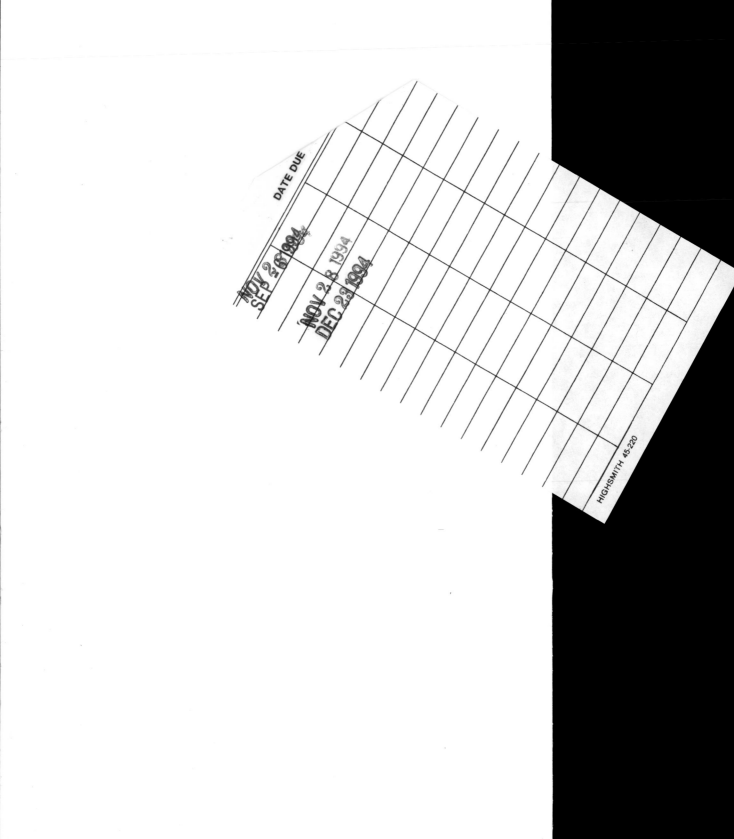